# Brittany Spaniel
# 20 Milestone Challenges

## Brittany Spaniel Memorable Moments. Includes Milestones for Memories, Gifts, Socialization & Training

Volume 1

---

Todays Doggy

Copyright © 2023

All rights reserved. Without limiting rights under the copyright reserved above, no part of this publication may be reproduced, stored, introduced into a retrieval system, distributed or transmitted in any form or by any means, including without limitation photocopying, recording, or other electronic or mechanical methods, without the prior written permission of the publisher, except in the case of brief quotations embodied in critical reviews and certain other non-commercial uses permitted by copyright law.

The scanning, uploading, and/or distribution of this document via the internet or via any other means without the permission of the publisher is illegal and is punishable by law. Please purchase only authorized editions and do not participate in or encourage electronic piracy of copyrightable materials

Dedicated To All of You Wonderful Owners and Fans

# Introduction

Welcome to the Original Doggy Milestone Series™ where you are encouraged to create those special moments with your dog. We have composed the milestones in a way that challenges you to set the stage before taking your photos.

Use props and make it fun - be creative in setting up your photos. Get family and friends involved - take it out with you - use it in different places and settings - have a play with it and most importantly, have a good time!

You can either hold the desired milestone spread open yourself - or have somebody hold it open as you take the snap.

If you would like to have the selected milestone book spread open and standing independently in your photos, you can use one or two large 'foldback' clips to hold the spread open.

Good luck and enjoy your photo fun.

# I Love My Family...

# ...And My Family Loves Me

# At The Beach!

# Having a Wave of a Time

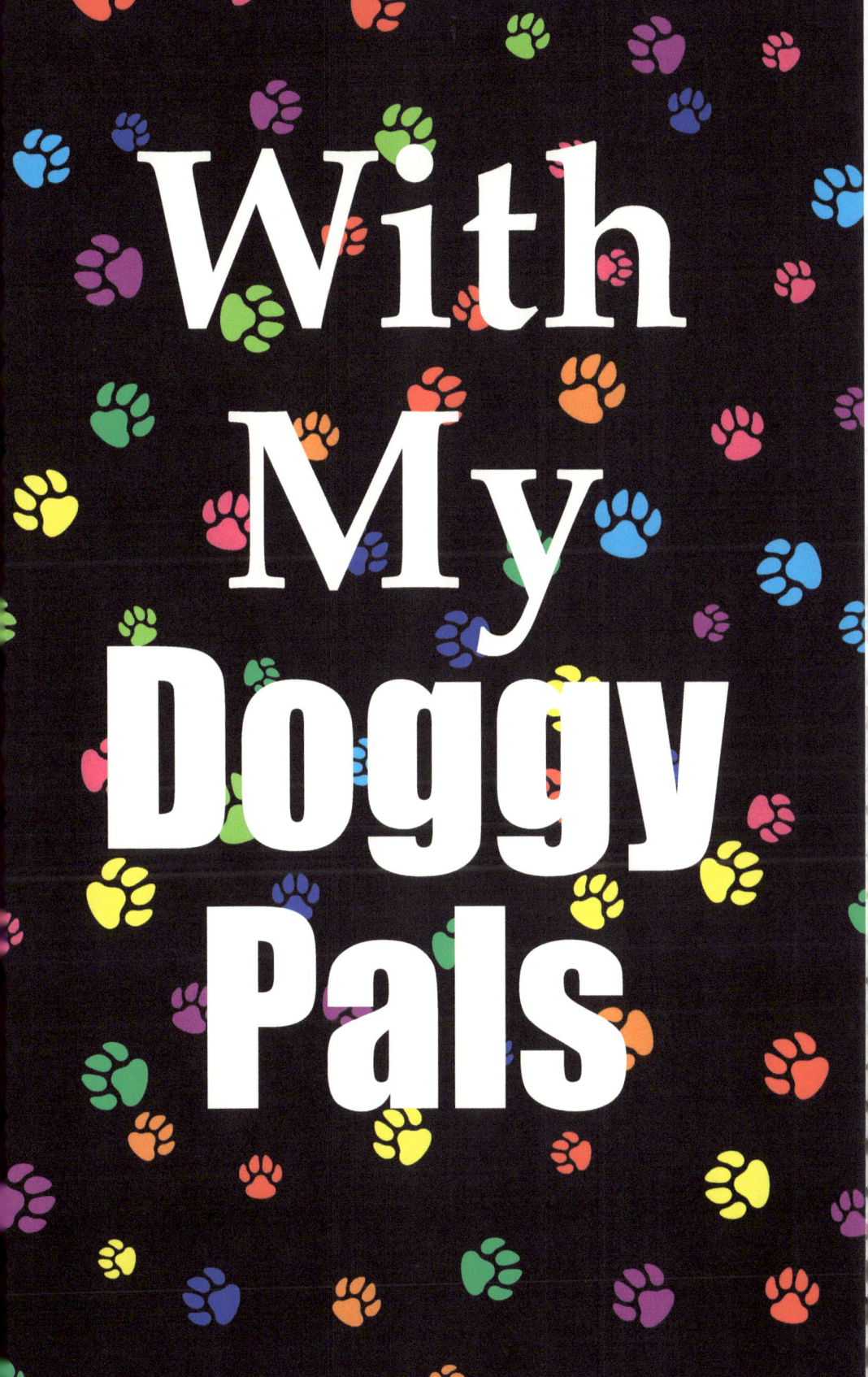

# IT'S...

# BED
# TIME

# I DIDN'T KNOW WHICH STICK YOU THREW

# SO I BOUGHT BACK ALL OF THEM

# I Need a HUGe

# OFF To The VET??

# CATCH ME IF YOU CAN!

# NASA Wants To Hire Me

# Because I'm a STAR!

# OOPS!
# I Buried Your Stuff

# ...But I Forgot Where

# Very Incredible Pup

# I DIDN'T DO IT

# I'll Just Be Over Here...

# Looking Fabulous

# PLEASE

# PLEASE

# PRETTY PLEEEASE

# CAN I KEEP IT?

# I'm On a SEAFOOD Diet

www.ingramcontent.com/pod-product-compliance
Lightning Source LLC
Chambersburg PA
CBHW041509010526
44118CB00006B/201